Language Arts Games

(Abridged from *Games to Improve Your Child's English*)

by ABRAHAM B. HURWITZ and

ARTHUR GODDARD

D1377792

SCHOLASTIC BOOK SERVICES
NEW YORK · TORONTO · LONDON · AUCKLAND · SYDNEY · TOKYO

To children, who learn through play,
This book has useful things to say.

Copyright © 1972, 1969 by Abraham B. Hurwitz and Arthur
Goddard. This abridged edition is published by Scholastic Book
Services, a division of Scholastic Magazines, Inc., by arrangement
with Simon & Schuster, Inc.

1st printing .... October 1972

Printed in the U. S. A.

Contents

Introduction

More and more, teachers are recognizing the highly motivational role of games in the effective learning of various subject skills. Well devised games stimulate children to think, reason, and concentrate. Repetition and drills are fun when they take the form of games that provide immediate goals. Children learn to work together as teams and to compete on a friendly basis. A pleasant, positive classroom atmosphere is generated in which learning and "work" are enjoyable.

This book provides a wide variety of carefully devised, ingenious, and relevant games which you can draw on to help your students master language skills. Developing proficiency in word usage is approached at different levels of maturity and in a variety of ways. The games are divided into four sections: rhyming games, vocabulary-building games, alphabet and spelling games, and grammar and sentence-construction games. Each game also contains many other aspects of language arts. All the games have been classroom tested.

To help you select those games which will best help you achieve your particular goals, the following information is given for each game: general level of the game, number of participants, materials necessary, and purpose of the game.

LEVELS OF MATURITY

Although it is impossible to ascribe a precise age level to each game, the authors have indicated levels of maturity as follows:

A. **Elementary** — chiefly for slower fourth and fifth graders.
B. **Intermediate** — for average fourth, fifth, and sixth graders.
C. **Elementary-Intermediate** — includes both slower and average fourth, fifth, and sixth graders.
D. **Intermediate-Advanced** — slightly harder than Intermediate.
E. **Advanced** — a range extending beyond Intermediate-Advanced, for bright students.
F. **All Levels** — may be used with any age group.

Note: These levels are flexible. And every game can be adjusted to fit the needs of your students. If it is too difficult, simpler words can be used, or the rules can be relaxed. If a game seems too easy for the class, use harder words and follow the suggestions and variations included for escalating the level. However, if a game, even with adjustments, seems too easy or too difficult, change to a new game. Do not overplay any game — stop before the children get tired of it. Encourage responses and correct any mistakes you can. The children should be encouraged to check themselves with a dictionary.

NUMBER OF PLAYERS

These are listed under each game. The games in this book fall into two groups: those suitable for the entire class (described as *2 or more* or *large groups*); and those for small groups of two and three (described as *2 only*), for independent activity time.

DESCRIPTION OF SKILLS TAUGHT

At the beginning of each game is a brief description of the skill it teaches. An Index of Skills Taught is given at the back of the book to aid you in locating a game on a particular skill which you may wish your class to work on.

MATERIALS

For most of the games you will need no materials. Some require cards that can be written on. These can be made by pasting stickers on the face of old playing cards, or by cutting 3″ x 5″ index cards in half. Each game gives the number of cards needed and the kinds of letters or words needed. Some games recommend a timer, but this is optional.

I

Games with Rhymes

Rhyme Whirl

Elementary-Intermediate   *Timer*

2 *or more*   *Wheel and spinning pointer*

This game teaches children a wide variety of rhymes and rhyming words, and improves reading by aiding in the recognition of common consonant blends. It also calls attention to the differences and similarities in the sounds of words.

Preparation

1. Using a compass, draw on white paper two separate circles, one somewhat smaller than the other. Follow the diagram for size and markings at regular intervals. Along the inside rim of the larger circle, write a number of consonant blends like BL, BR, CL, CR, DR, FL, FR, GL, GR, GH, KN, PL, PR, SC, SCH, SH, SL, SR, ST, STR, SW, TH, THR, TR, SN, SM, WH, etc. Then cut this larger circle which will become the outer disk.

2. Along the inside rim of the smaller circle write a number of simple word endings like AT, AM, IP, AND, OP, ING, IM, OWN, ANCE, UM, OD, OOP, OOL, AZE,

INK, ANK, OKE, OCK, UN, ITE, IPE, ICK, ACT, IKE, IDE, etc. These should correspond with the markings on the larger wheel. This will be the inside disk.

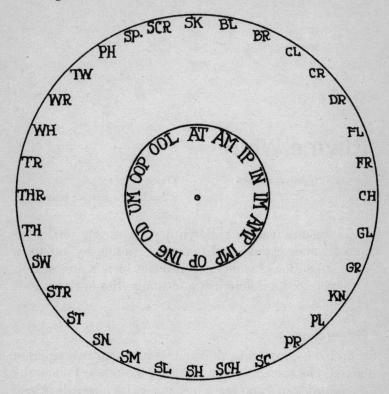

3. Paste each disk to cardboard backing, and trim the cardboard. Insert a two-pronged paper fastener through the center of both disks. Now, open the prongs and press them flat, so that the smaller disk freely twirls on top of the larger disk.

How to Play

The players take turns twirling the center disk to line

up word endings with different consonant blends. Each player attempts to line up any two of the combinations that make a word. For example, suppose that a player lines up IM with TR, to make TRIM. Now, within a given time, he must name as many words as he can that rhyme with *trim* — *slim, him, grim, gym, whim, prim, brim, skim, vim, hymn, limb, rim,* etc. As can be seen from these examples, what counts is the *rhyme,* not the spelling. Thus, words like *praise, prays,* and *maize* could be cited as rhymes for *glaze* on the rhyme whirl.

A player receives one point for each rhyming word he names within a given time limit. If, after twirling the disk, a player cannot find any combination that makes a word, he loses his turn to the next player. He is allowed to choose a combination that has been previously used, but he may not repeat a rhyming word already given. (To check this, you or a student can record the rhyming words as they are given.) The child with the greatest number of points wins the game.

You can make and keep in reserve a number of additional center disks with different rhyme endings. These can be easily substituted to help vary the game or to make it more difficult.

Rhyme Wheel

Elementary-Intermediate
2 or more

Blackboard and chalk
Timer
Wheel and spinning pointer

In this variation of RHYME WHIRL, the players build rhymes from given endings found by twirling a pointer on a wheel like that shown on page 14.

Preparation

Here only one circle is needed. Around and within its circumference you can place rhyme endings of varying difficulty — e.g., END, ABLE, IPE, ACT, ICK, IF, ORN, ORT, AWL, OOL, EAK, OKE, etc.

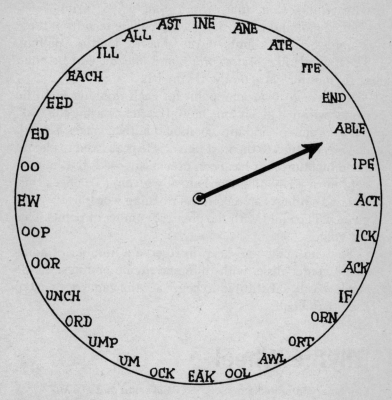

How to Play

Each player, in turn, gets one spin. He must then name as many words as he can, within a given time, that contain the rhyme with the sound of the ending to which the spinner points. For example, if he gets OKE, he might say *"Joke, cloak, croak, smoke, poke, spoke, and oak"* before time is up. Each of these words would then count as one point in his credit. The teacher or best speller writes all words on the blackboard for the other players to see.

Now, if he or another player again spins the pointer to OKE, no credit could be given for any of the words already listed. New rhymes would have to be thought of — perhaps *yolk, folk, revoke, soak, broke,* and *woke.* In this way, all the players are kept on their toes and learn new words and rhymes for one another.

Finally, after every player has just about exhausted his stock of rhymes for the endings shown on the wheel, the list under each should be looked at by all and compared with the lists under these endings to be found in a rhyming dictionary.

Rhyme Concentration

All Levels   *Blank cards*
2 *only*

This card game can be used to review familiar rhymes and to introduce new rhymes and rhyming words. It requires concentration and a retentive memory.

Preparation

1. Prepare a deck of cards arranged in matched pairs of rhyming words. (Decks may also be made of matched triplets or of quadruplets for more advanced classes.) The rhymes and the words to be selected for the cards will depend on what is to be taught or reviewed, and what level of difficulty is desired. They may include such easy and obvious matches as *pore* and *sore, dear* and *clear, life* and *wife, tea* and *sea,* and *rose* and *pose;* or, at an inter-

mediate level, such words as *tough* and *puff, plough* and *now, crude* and *stewed,* and *taught* and *thought.* Triplets and quadruplets can contain words of different degrees of difficulty — e.g., *spoon, hewn,* and *commune* or *quicker, liquor, knicker,* and *vicar.*

2. The number of cards in the deck will depend on the players' ability to concentrate. Too much strain is placed on the memory of each player if more than forty-eight cards are used. This number, divisible by two, three, and four, lends itself to various combinations of pairs, triplets, and quadruplets. However, extra sets of cards with different rhyming words can be kept in reserve for later rounds.

How to Play

Shuffle the cards and spread them out face down on the table. The first player picks up two cards at random and shows them to his opponent. If the cards match — i.e., if they make a rhyme, like *gamble* and *ramble* — the first player lays them face *up* on his side of the table and scores one point. He then gets another chance to find a matching pair by picking up two more cards. If he fails to do so, he must return *one* of the cards he has picked up (after showing both to his opponent), face down, to its former place on the table. He keeps the other card in his hand and, when his turn next comes, draws only one card.

The second player now picks a card from those lying face down on the table and shows it to his opponent. He then tries to recall the wording and the position of the card that was put down by his opponent, in order to determine whether the word on it will rhyme with the one on the card in his hand. If he remembers that they do *not* rhyme, he may choose any other card. If, either through good memory or good luck, he succeeds in getting a rhyming pair of words, he lays both cards, face up, on his side of the table. Thus he scores a point and gets another chance to find a matching pair. Whenever a card is drawn from the table, it must be shown to the other player in order to give that player a chance to memorize its wording and position in case it is laid down again and is later wanted.

The game proceeds in this way until the last card has been drawn from the table, whether at random or because a player recalled its wording and location. The winner is the player with the highest score.

When playing with rhyming triplets or quadruplets, if a player draws a card that rhymes with a pair laid down previously by his opponent, to form a triplet, he may take his opponent's pair, add his own rhyming word, put the whole triplet on his own side of the table, and draw again. Similarly, his opponent may win back the triplet if he can draw the rhyming card that makes it a quadruplet. If a player draws a card that rhymes with any pair or triplet on his own side of the table, he adds it to his collection and draws again. In each case, the player adds a point to his score.

The game can be made increasingly difficult by inserting sets of harder rhyming words in successive rounds.

Fishing for Rhymes

Elementary-Intermediate   *Blank cards*
2 *or more*

This game will teach children to recognize rhymes,

acquaint them with common ones, and build their vocabulary.

Preparation

1. A deck of cards must first be prepared. Each card is to have on it a different word, but the words selected should form rhymed sets of two, three, or more. The words should be suited to the interests and maturity of the players and should include some new vocabulary for them.

2. At least fifty-two cards — i.e., twenty-six pairs of rhymes — should be used. Extra sets of cards can be reserved to increase the difficulty in successive rounds after the players have become familiar with the easier one-syllable rhymes.

3. The cards are thoroughly shuffled, and five are dealt to each player, one at a time per round, the remainder being placed face down on the table.

How to Play

Beginning with the player on the dealer's left, each player, in turn, one at a time, asks any other player for a card that rhymes with a particular word he already has. He says, "Please give me a word that rhymes with _____."

If the player addressed has one or more cards with such a word, he must give them all to the one who asked for them. The latter may then continue to ask any other player for the cards he wants as long as he is successful. If he cannot get the card he wants from the player he addresses, he is told to "Go fish," and he must draw the top card from the deck lying face down on the table. If this card completes a set of rhymed words, he may lay it down, and he gets another chance to draw, until he is

18

unable to obtain a rhyming set. Then the turn to play passes to the next player at the left.

As a player succeeds in obtaining sets of rhymes, he shows them to the others and lays them face down in front of him. When there are no more cards left in the deck, the round is over, and the player with the most sets of rhymes wins. Ten points are scored for winning each round.

If a player has a card that is called for but denies having it when asked, he is penalized one point for each player in the game.

Ad-Verse

All Levels
2 or more

This game can be played endlessly. It provides further practice in simple versifying.

How to Play

The first player begins by telling a little story in rhymed verse. The last line of this verse must end with a reference to something present, absent, found, lost, bought, or sold. The next player must then add two rhymed lines to the story. In the first line, he must say something about the object the first player mentioned. In the second line, he must introduce a new object. The game proceeds in this way until the chain is broken by a player's failure to supply the "missing link." In that case, the player who cannot supply the link may challenge the preceding player to do so. If his AD-VERSary can supply the link, he scores two points; if he cannot, he is penalized two points. One point is scored for each added link.

Here is how one such chain of rhymes began:

Player 1:   I went downtown
To see Mr. Brown.
He gave me a nickel
To buy a pickle.

Player 2:   The pickle was sour;
So I bought a flower.

Player 1:   The flower was dead;
So I got some bread.

Player 2:   The bread was stale;
So I bought a pail.

Player 1:   The pail was small;
So I got a ball.

Player 2:   The ball was hard;
So I bought some lard.

Player 1:   The lard was thick;
So I found a stick.

Children will carry on a game like this indefinitely, meanwhile thinking up a host of rhymes.

Crumb Crambo

Intermediate-Advanced
Large groups

This well-known game teaches children rhymes, builds vocabulary, and encourages originality and inventiveness.

How to Play

The players are divided into two evenly matched teams. With one team out of the room, the other decides on some verb — preferably one with which many words rhyme — that can be acted out or pantomimed. Suppose, for example, that the team chooses the word *fight*. When the other group returns, they are told that the word rhymes with *might*. Once more the other group leaves the room to decide among themselves what they think the word is. Suppose they think the word is *write*. When they return, without speaking they act out this word, some by making silent scribbling motions, others by pantomiming the use of pen or pencil, etc. The other group must then decide whether the correct verb has been guessed. If they decide it has not, they shake their heads. Neither side may say a word.

The game proceeds in this way until the correct word has been guessed and acted out. Then the team that chose the word claps their hands, and it is their turn to leave the room while their opponents select another word.

II

Vocabulary-Building Games

Words are the pegs to hang ideas on.
— HENRY WARD BEECHER

Abbreviation Crossroads

Elementary-Intermediate
2 or more, or large groups

Graph paper and colors
pencil
Timer

This game teaches children the meaning of common abbreviations.

Preparation

The graph shown is drawn on the blackboard, if a large group is playing. If a small group is playing, it is drawn on paper. (See page 26.)

How to Play

The first player closes his eyes and puts his chalk point on the board. If the chalk touches a line, the player misses his chance, and it is the next player's turn to try. If the chalk touches a box, the player shades it in. Then he must try to make as many meaningful abbreviations as he can with the six letters with which that box is aligned vertically, horizontally, and diagonally.

For each letter in his abbreviations he scores one point.

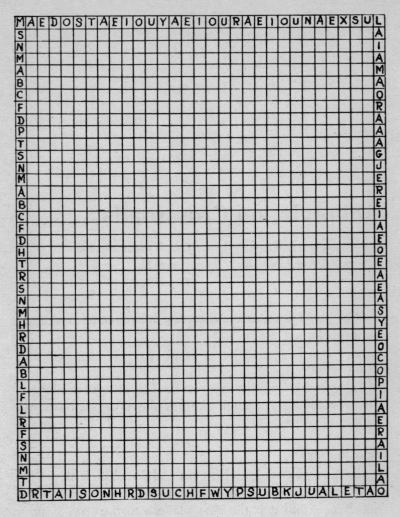

Succeeding players follow the same procedure. If a player touches a box that has already been marked, he gets two additional chances to "hit" an empty box. The game ends either within a set time or when all the boxes have been marked.

26

A dictionary should be readily available to settle disputed points.

Don't Miss a Word!

Intermediate-Advanced   *Timer*
2 *or more*

This game adds words to the players' vocabulary at the same time that it teaches them spelling.

How to Play

The first player, thinking of a word beginning with the prefix MIS, provides a clue to its meaning by asking a question starting with "What sort of Miss . . . ?" The next player must then, within a given time, guess what the word is. If he does so, he must think of another word beginning with MIS and likewise provide the succeeding player with a clue to its meaning. The game proceeds in this way, with players dropping out as they are unable to guess the word or think of new words beginning with the same prefix. The winner is the player who survives this process of elimination.

Here is how the game might begin:

Player 1: What sort of Miss is an error?
Player 2: A mistake. What sort of Miss hurts business?
Player 1: Mismanagement. What sort of Miss is not a Miss at all?

Player 2:	A mister. What sort of Miss gets you into trouble with the law?
Player 1:	A misdemeanor. What sort of Miss destroys a nation?
Player 2:	Misrule. What sort of Miss prompts a kiss?
Player 1:	Mistletoe. What sort of Miss is out of place?
Player 2:	A misfit. What sort of Miss flies through the air?
Player 1:	A missile. What sort of Miss has the wrong name?
Player 2:	A misnomer.

Variations

Although all the words used here are nouns, the game can also be played with verbs beginning with the same prefix if the question is put in the form "How do you miss when you . . . ?" For example, a game might proceed in this way:

Player 1:	How do you miss when you lead someone astray?
Player 2:	Misguide. How do you miss when you lose things?
Player 1:	Mislay. How do you miss when you lead someone astray?
Player 2:	We had that already. Misguide.
Player 1:	No. Misdirect. How do you miss when you waste money?
Player 2:	Misspend. How do you miss when you don't understand?
Player 1:	Misconstrue or misunderstand. How do you miss when your orthography is all wrong?
Player 2:	Misspell.

Iceman

Intermediate   *Timer*
2 or more

This is an ICE way to learn some new words and their spelling.

How to Play

This game is played like DON'T MISS A WORD! except that the cue is given by asking "What kind of ice . . . ?" Here is how a game might begin:

Player 1:   What kind of ice would the world be better off without?
Player 2:   Vice. What kind of ice is used as a seasoning?
Player 3:   Spice. What kind of ice is seen at weddings?
Player 1:   Rice. What kind of ice is easier to give than to take?
Player 2:   Advice. What kind of ice do cats relish?
Player 3:   Mice. What kind of ice do you gamble with?
Player 1:   Dice.

Among other words that can be used in this game are *lice, twice, thrice, slice, splice, device, paradise, precise, sacrifice, price, trice,* etc.

Categories

Intermediate-Advanced   *Paper and pencil*
2 or more   *Timer*

This is the classic game for building vocabulary. It is an

ideal way of encouraging students to notice the things around them and to learn their names. By training them to group items logically in their correct classification, this game also contributes to the development of an orderly mind.

Since a premium is placed on knowing unusual words not likely to be thought of by other players, almost everybody who participates learns some new words when the results are pooled and the answers are compared.

How to Play

First, each player is asked, in turn, to name a category, such as fruits, flowers, vegetables, animals, birds, fish, colors, fabrics, tools, boats, trees, gems, countries, authors, meats, etc. As these are named, each player lists them vertically in a column at the left.

Then the players agree on some word of five letters — say, HANDS. This is spelled out, spaced across the top of the page, starting just to the right of the list of categories, to form a rectangular chart with boxes wide enough to accommodate fairly long words. (This basic pattern might be dittoed ahead of time.)

Now, each player, within a given time, has to fill in the boxes by finding in every category a word that begins with the letter at the top of the column.

On top of page 31, for instance, is the way one such chart might look.

Plenty of time should be allowed so that most of the boxes will be filled in. Then the papers are exchanged for scoring. A player reads aloud the first word on the paper before him, and the other players check to see whether it is duplicated on theirs. If the word is correct, the player who thought of it receives as many points as there are other players who did *not* have it on their papers. Thus,

	H	A	N	D	S
FRUITS	HUCKLEBERRY	APPLE	NECTARINE	DATES	STRAWBERRY
TREES	HEMLOCK	ASPEN	NUTMEG	DOGWOOD	SUMAC
FLOWERS	HYACINTH	AZALEA	NARCISSUS	DAISY	SWEET PEA
TOOLS	HATCHET	AX	NIPPERS	DIVIDER	SAW
FABRICS	HAIRCLOTH	ACETATE	NYLON	DENIM	SILK
ANIMALS	HAMSTER	ALLIGATOR	NEWT	DONKEY	SHEEP

if five are playing the game, and only one thought of
acetate, that word would be worth four points; but if two
players had thought of it, each of them would be credited
with three points for it. The same procedure is followed
with each word, and the player who scores the most points
wins.

With this system of scoring, a player who wanted to
avoid the common tool *saw,* which others might think of,
might write, instead, *scyth, sickle, shovel, stapler,* or
spatula. If he doesn't think of these, others might; so that,
when the results are compared, almost everybody learns
some new words.

Ghost

All Levels   *Timer*
2 or more

This is the classic word game that almost everybody has
played at one time or another.

How to Play

The first player, thinking of any word of more than three letters, calls out just its first letter. Then the second player, thinking perhaps of the same word or some other word of at least four letters, adds a second letter. Each succeeding player must think of a word that begins with the letters already called out and must add one letter, but he must avoid completing any word.

Generally, only one minute is allowed for a player either to add a letter or to challenge the preceding player to say what word he had in mind. If the preceding player cannot meet this challenge, either because he really had no word in mind or because he cannot spell it correctly, he is penalized by becoming "a fifth of a ghost." If he does meet the challenge successfully, then it is his challenger who is so penalized. A player suffers the same penalty if he completes a word of four or more letters and someone else points this out.

A second penalty makes a player two fifths of a ghost, and so on, until five penalties make one a whole ghost. No surviving player may speak to a ghost during the course of the game. Anyone who does becomes a ghost too. Naturally, ghosts are free to do their best to elicit remarks from the surviving players. The winner is the one player who is left at the end.

Suppose, for example, that the first player, thinking of the word *aunt,* calls out "A." The second player, thinking perhaps of *agreeable,* will call out "G." The third player, thinking of *agape,* will call out "A." The fourth player, thinking of *against,* will add "I." Now the fifth player finds that he cannot think of any words other than *again* and *against* that begin with this combination of letters. For either of these he would have to add an N and thus complete a word. He would then become "a fifth of a ghost."

As a rule, proper names, foreign words, and abbreviations are prohibited.

Superghost

Intermediate-Advanced   *Timer*

2 or more

This is the more modern and more complicated variation of GHOST. It is also called FORE-AND-AFT GHOST or HEADS-AND-TAILS GHOST. It is an ideal way of introducing a child to the common prefixes.

How to Play

The rules are the same as GHOST, except that a player may add a letter *either before or after* the ones already called out. In short, one can spell backward or forward from any point. Again, only words of four or more letters count.

In both SUPERGHOST and GHOST, a knowledge of prefixes can frequently help a player to avoid adding a letter that completes a word. For example, suppose a player's turn comes when the letters *fac* have been given. To avoid making the complete words *face* or *fact*, he might add either an I after the C (for *facing*) or an E before the F (for *preface*). If he puts an F before the F (for *efface*), he also successfully avoids being turned into part of a ghost.

Should this game prove too great a strain on the memory, players may be permitted to use paper and pencil to keep a record of the letters called out.

Graphic Ghost

All Levels
2 or more, or large groups

Paper and pencil
Graph paper and colored
pencil

This is a quiet variation of GHOST. It teaches spelling and improves vocabulary.

Preparation

Draw a square, like the one shown on top of page 35, consisting of about two hundred and twenty-five boxes, with fifteen boxes on each side.

How to Play

The first player thinks of a word. He then writes its first letter in the box at the upper left corner. His opponent, also thinking of some word, adds the necessary letter to the one already written, proceeding horizontally. The players then take turns adding letters in this manner. A player loses one point if he cannot state the word he has in mind when he is challenged to do so. If he completes a word, he loses another point. When one of the players has lost five points, his opponent wins the game.

(If SUPERGHOST is played graphically, the letters must be placed precisely in the box in which they belong, leaving space before and after for the missing letters of the word).

Variations

More difficult variations can also be tried. For example, the players might attempt to build vertically, moving downward, from the letters of a given word or part of a word written horizontally. In that case too, SUPERGHOST

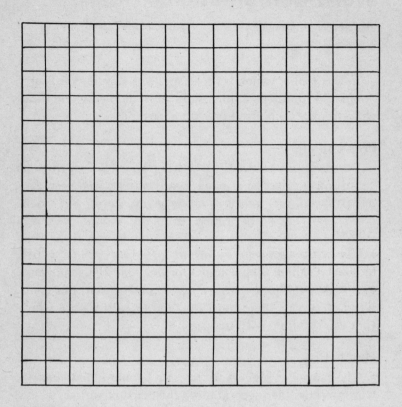

can be played graphically by placing letters in the vertical row in which they belong and leaving space below for the missing letters of the word. If a square of fifteen boxes on each side proves too small, the grid can be extended in any direction to suit the needs of the game.

(GRAPHIC GHOST can also be played by more than two players if the grid is placed on a blackboard. Then the players can take turns chalking in the letters of the words they have in mind).

Word Combinations

Elementary-Intermediate   *Blank cards*

1 or more

In this game, which teaches spelling, simple words are composed from still simpler ones. It is an ideal game for a child to play by himself or with a classmate.

Preparation

Prepare a set of cards by writing on each a word that could form a part of a longer word — e.g., *stick, tar, be, off, ball, am, ice, get, sea, house, store, horse,* etc. Such words can easily be found in many words of three syllables or more, like *together, incapable, gasoline, lieutenant, diploma, cockatoo, origin,* and even in some words of two syllables, like *palled, fortune, message, current, grammar, brandish, hermit, mayor,* and *season.* For each word on a card there must be another card with a word that can combine with it.

How to Play

The player or players try to form as many new, longer words as possible by combining the cards in various ways. Thus, words that might be built with the elements listed here are *beam, target, office,* etc.

Variations

1. In a larger group, each child can be given a big card with only a part of a word, like *ind.* Then he must find his "mate" with the other part — the child who holds up the letters *ian.* Children who make up a complete word then line up with their cards.

2. The game can be further complicated if a long word,

like *penmanship,* is broken up into three parts, each of
which is a word in itself: *pen, man,* and *ship.*

Sillygisms

Intermediate-Advanced   *Timer*
2 *or more*

This game, an adaptation of WORD COMBINATIONS,
helps children to appreciate the humor of the situation
and lightens the tension involved in learning to spell.

The best way to understand the game is to examine a
typical sillygism:

"This is a pew. This is a pill. Therefore, this is a pupil."

The idea is to build up a word by putting together
syllables that have the sound of other, logically unrelated
words. In short, the word so constructed must *not* consist
of a combination like *sawdust, coattail,* or *baseball,* in
which two or more words are logically joined together to
form a compound. The words should have no connection
whatever — for example, *mop* and *pet (moppet).*

How to Play

The first player, thinking of some sillygism, calls out
only the first sentence — say, "This is an inn."

Now the second player must try to determine what
word the first player had in mind or perhaps think of a
word himself. If he cannot do so, he may challenge the
first player to complete the sillygism. One point is earned
for thinking of the complete sillygism, and one point for
spelling each of the words of which it consists. (This
particular one continues as follows: "This is a turn. Therefore, this is an intern." *Inn, turn,* and *intern* would have to

be correctly spelled.) If a player is challenged to complete his sillygism, he is penalized two points if he cannot do so. Mispronunciations are likewise penalized, like *soup, purse, stitch, us (superstitious)*.

Here is how one game proceeded:

Player 1: This is a pan.
Player 2: This is a tree. Therefore, this is a pantry.
Player 3: This is a pan.
Player 1: We just had that one. It's a pantry.
Player 3: No, this is a nick. Therefore, this is a panic.
Player 2: This is a miss.
Player 3: This is a sill. Therefore, this is a missile.
Player 1: This is a sea.
Player 2: This is a son. Therefore, this is a season.
Player 3: No good! You have a mispronounciation. Minus one point for you! This is a seed. Therefore, this is secede.

(Here a verb has been used instead of a noun. Allowing different parts of speech adds to the instructiveness of the game.)

Player 1: This is a tail.
Player 2: This is an oar. Therefore, this is a tailor.
Player 3: This is a tack.
Player 1: This is tic. Therefore, this is a tactic.
Player 2: This is an ax.
Player 3: This is a scent. Therefore, this is an accent.
Player 1: This is a part.
Player 2: This is a tea. Therefore, this is a party.
Player 3: This is rust.
Player 1: This is a tick. Therefore, this is a rustic.
Player 1: This is a pate.
Player 3: This is a run. Therefore, this is a patron.

The game can continue with sillygisms like *pat* and *tee* (*patty*), *tine* and *knee* (*tiny*), *ants* and *sir* (*answer*), *vest* and *tree* (*vestry*), *wind* and *doe* (*window*), and *prod* and *duct* (*product*).

Variation

At a more difficult level the same game can be played with sillygisms forming three-syllable words, like *fan* and *attic* (*fanatic*) or *paw* and *city* (*paucity*).

Can You Do It?

Intermediate-Advanced
2 or more

This is another game with compound words that can be played just for laughs.

How to Play

Each player, in turn, must ask a silly question involving a play on a compound word. The humor is in the realization that one part of the compound has another meaning entirely in a different context.

Here, for example, is how one such game proceeded:

Player 1:   Can you see a bed spread?
Player 2:   Can you make a pillow fight?
Player 3:   Can you wake a sleeping car?
Player 1:   Can you see a pipe dream?
Player 2:   Can you see a home stretch?
Player 3:   Can you make a bed roll?
Player 1:   Can you make a bell hop?

Player 2:	Can you see a shoe box?
Player 3:	Can you make a sack race?
Player 1:	Can you see a dress parade?
Player 2:	Can you see a fire escape?
Player 3:	Can you see a salad dressing?
Player 1:	Can you make a garden fence?
Player 2:	Can you see a nose dive?
Player 3:	Can you see a cake walk?
Player 1:	Can you make a wolf pack?
Player 2:	Can you see a fox trot?
Player 3:	Can you see a horse fly?
Player 1:	Can you make a whip saw?
Player 2:	Can you make a board walk?
Player 3:	Can you make a room mate?
Player 1:	Can you see a fish bowl?
Player 2:	Can you hear an ear drum?
Player 3:	Can you see a walking stick?
Player 1:	Can you blow a shoe horn?
Player 2:	Can you hear a cigar band?
Player 3:	Can you hear a tree bark?
Player 1:	Can you put on the gloves with a boxing match?
Player 2:	Can you make a jury box?
Player 3:	Can you see a hand spring?
Player 1:	Can you watch a roller skate?
Player 2:	Can you make a band stand?
Player 3:	Can you see a clam bake?
Player 1:	Can you see a kitchen sink?
Player 2:	Can you suggest clothes suitable for a dressing room?
Player 3:	Can you make a house hold?
Player 1:	Can you make a bed spring?
Player 2:	Can you lift a light house?
Player 3:	Can you make wood work?

Synonym Match

Intermediate-Advanced   *Timer*

2 or more

This game adds synonyms to the child's vocabulary and increases the verbal resources he has at his command for immediate recall and use.

How to Play

The first player calls out a word for which he knows at least one synonym. The next player must, within a given time, "match" the word by providing any synonym of it, and as many more as he can think of. He receives one point for each synonym he calls out. If he cannot think of any, he may challenge the first player to state what synonym he had in mind. Any failure in this respect is penalized one point to discourage the introduction of words that have no synonyms. A player fails to score a point if he is unable to think of a synonym, and he is penalized one point if he responds with a word that is not a synonym of the word proposed by the preceding player.

The object is to squeeze as many synonyms out of the original word as possible. If a player can think of only one or two, his opponent may add a few points to his score by thinking of some others. How far this process goes will depend, of course, on the abilities of the players and on the words they choose to begin with. If, for example, *fat* is the first word called out, the players might suggest *chubby, beefy, stocky, thick,* and *heavyset* before breaking down. A more advanced group might be able to go on to *portly, rotund, paunchy, obese, corpulent,* etc.

Variation

When the possibilities of a given word have been exhausted, a new one, preferably of a different part of speech (noun, verb, adverb, etc.) can be proposed. (A thesaurus should be kept handy to settle any disputed points).

Antonym Match

Intermediate-Advanced   *Timer*
2 or more

This game is the counterpart to SYNONYM MATCH. After the players have provided the synonyms of a word, they can learn its antonyms and extend their vocabulary still further.

How to Play

The game is played in the same way as SYNONYM MATCH, except that the players have to match antonyms.

Thus, if *fat* is the given word, the appropriate response might be *thin*. Now the next player might suggest an antonym of *thin* without using the word *fat*. In this way, the game builds on SYNONYM MATCH. For example, *chubby* might be matched by *lanky, paunchy* by *slender, beefy* by *slim, obese* by *lean,* and *portly* by *gaunt.*

Variations

1. At a more advanced level, this game can be used to teach children the prefixes that turn words into their antonyms: *ir, de, a, mis, dis, in, im, un,* etc., making words like *disappear, disservice, unmistakable, irreparable, decontrol, indivisible,* and *amoral.* The problem then be-

comes one of deciding whether to say *unsanitary* or *insanitary, immobile* or *unmobile,* and so forth. Similarly, children learn how to add suffixes like *less* (*hopeless*) and *ful* (*hopeful*) to form antonyms.

2. As with Synonym Match, different parts of speech can be used.

Homonym Match

Intermediate-Advanced   *Timer*
2 *only*

In this game the players learn to distinguish among homonyms by matching them in complete sentences in which they are used correctly.

How to Play

The first player forms a sentence in which he uses a word that he knows has a homonym. For example, he may begin by saying, "She will *sew* a dress."

The second player has to decide, within a given time, which word in that sentence has a homonym and then use the homonym correctly in a matching sentence of his own. He would be wrong, for example, if he said, "Is she still at the same *address?*" But he would be right and score a point if he said, "*So* what?" If he cannot think of a homonym to match his opponent's, he may challenge his opponent to supply a sentence with its appropriate matching homonym. Since there is a penalty of two points for failure to do so, the formation of sentences with words that have no homonyms is discouraged.

Let us follow this particular dialogue for a while:

Player 1:   I *know* it.

Player 2:   *No*, you don't. Didn't you *see* it?

Player 1:   Yes, it's floating on the *sea*. It's a *flea*.

Player 2:   Perhaps it's trying to *flee*. *I'll* see you later.

Player 1:   On a desert *isle* I suppose.

Players may begin with the easy and obvious combinations like *so, sew,* and *sow; rain, reign,* and *rein; rode, road,* and *rowed; meat, meet,* and *mete;* and proceed to more difficult ones like *necklace* and *neckless; patience* and *patients; plum* and *plumb; praise, prays,* and *preys; feign, fain,* and *fane; gate* and *gait; gorilla* and *guerrilla; ewes* and *yews;* and *sight, cite,* and *site.*

Other words with homonyms that some players may have difficulty in spelling or using are *sink, combing, carrot, symbol, core, nice, new, grieves, pair, mean, gambol, yolk,* and *straight.*

Concentration

All Levels   *Blank cards*
2 *only*

This versatile game can be used to teach synonyms, antonyms, homonyms, common phrases, or any desired combination of them. As its name indicates, it promotes concentration and requires a good memory.

Preparation

1. A deck of cards, arranged in matched pairs, is prepared by the teacher. The pairs of words selected for the

cards will depend on what is to be taught and the level of difficulty desired. Thus, if antonyms are to be matched, cards may include, at the elementary level, pairs like *fat* and *skinny, stop* and *go, night* and *day, short* and *tall,* and correspondingly more difficult pairs at a more advanced level. If common phrases are to be matched, the cards may include *spick* and *span, ham* and *eggs, willy* and *nilly, touch* and *go, to* and *fro,* etc.

2. The number of cards in the deck will depend on the players' powers of concentration. A great strain is placed on their memory if more than forty cards — i.e., twenty pairs — are used at one time, but extra sets with different pairs of words can be kept in reserve for successive rounds.

How to Play

All the cards, after being thoroughly shuffled, are spread out, helter-skelter, face down on the table. The first player then picks up two cards at random and shows them to his opponent. If the cards match — i.e., if they make an appropriate pair (synonyms, antonyms, homonyms, etc.) — the first player places them face up on his side of the table and scores one point. He may then have another try at finding a matching pair. If he cannot do so, he must return one of them, after showing both to his opponent, face down, to its former place.

The second player now picks one card at random from those lying face down on the table. He tries to remember the position and the wording of the card that was put down by his opponent in order to determine whether it will match the card in his hand. If, either through luck in picking up his second card or through correctly remembering the location of the card he needs, he succeeds in getting a matched pair, he lays both cards down, face up, on his side of the table, scores one point, and draws again.

If, at this point, the second player has used the first player's discard, the second player now draws two cards. At all times, a card that is picked up from the table must be shown to one's opponent in order to give him a chance to memorize its location in case it is put down again.

The game proceeds in this way until the last card has been picked up from the table. The winner is the player with the highest score.

Complications can be added by gradually raising the level of difficulty in matching words in successive rounds and increasing, a pair at a time, the number of cards in the deck with each round.

Teakettle

Intermediate-Advanced
Large groups

This old favorite is an excellent game for teaching the difference in meaning between homonyms.

How to Play

One player, the victim, goes out of the room, while the rest of the players agree on a pair of homonyms. When the victim returns, he asks each player a question in an effort to determine what the homonyms are. The responses must be so phrased as to require the use of either one of the homonyms, but the word "teakettle" must be substituted for them. From these clues the victim must discover the words that "teakettle" stands for.

For example, suppose the homonyms chosen are *knows* and *nose*. The dialogue between the victim and his tormentors might proceed as follows:

Victim: Is it something you buy?
Player 1:   You can buy a false teakettle, but not the real teakettle.
Victim: Is it something you wear?
Player 2:   Everyone teakettles he has a teakettle, but you can't wear a real teakettle.
Victim: Is it something you do?
Player 3:   It's something you *can* do. Everyone here now teakettles but you!
Victim: Is it something in this room?
Player 4:   It's as plain as the teakettle on your face.
(After that clue, let us hope the victim knows his nose!)

Good sets of homonyms for this game are *pries* and *prize*, *pore* and *pour*, *would* and *wood*, *sail* and *sale*, *read* and *red*, *steal* and *steel*, *tail* and *tale*, *hour* and *our*, and *flour* and *flower*.

The game can be complicated by using the word "teakettle" to represent three words that are homonyms, like *cent*, *scent*, and *sent*, or *rode*, *road*, and *rowed*.

Variations

1. A variation of this game can be played by using "teakettle" to represent two entirely different meanings of the same word, such as *hind* (a deer and rear), *left*, *beam*, *part*, *fare*, *game*, *rose*, *safe*, *soil*, *stole*, etc.

2. For a grammatical variation of the same game, see COFFEEPOT (page 83).

Whistle Stop

All Levels   *Whistle*
Large groups   *Timer*

This game places a premium on alertness and mental swiftness. It teaches children to group ideas logically and can be used to build vocabulary in any field or subject — history, geography, science, music, etc.

How to Play

Instruct the children to listen carefully as you call out a series of four words. Before you blow your whistle, they must say which word does *not* fit in with the other three. A correct answer must be explained by the player who gives it if he is to score a point for it.

If there is a tie among the children, or if there is doubt about who spoke up first, runoffs can be held to see who is the quickest in finding the incongruity.

The game can be made increasingly difficult, as the following sequence of combinations shows:

Harp, violin, orchestra, drum.
Bat, flagpole, golf club, tennis racket.
Monkey, frog, giraffe, dog.
Atlantic, Pacific, Arctic, temperate.
Hat, handkerchief, gloves, trousers.
Sun, clouds, rain, fog.
Vixen, doe, drake, cow.
Shoes, floor, fingernails, furniture.

(You polish all four of the last, but only three of them begin with F.)

Variations

Other ways of complicating the game are to make sets

with synonyms, antonyms, homonyms, and different parts of speech, or to add to the number of items in each series.

Blow the Whistle

Elementary-Intermediate   *Whistle*
Large groups   *Timer*

Like WHISTLE STOP, this game demands a speedy response. It is essentially a game of word association designed to familiarize children with common groups of three words each.

How to Play

Instruct the children to listen carefully as you call out a series of two words. Before you blow your whistle, they must add the third word that completes the group.

In case of a tie or doubt about who answered first, a runoff should be held.

Here, for example, are some sets that can be used in this game:

Red, white, and ——————— .
Sun, moon, and ——————— .
Ready, set, ——————— .
Tom, Dick, and ——————— .
Hook, line, and ——————— .
Man, woman, and ——————— .
Stop, look, and ——————— .
Lock, stock, and ——————— .
Healthy, wealthy, and ——————— .
Deaf, dumb, and ——————— .
Hop, skip, and ——————— .

Reading, writing, and ——————— .
Faith, hope, and ——————— .
Morning, noon, and ——————— .
Wine, women, and ——————— .
Knife, fork, and ——————— .
Ear, nose, and ——————— .
Ready, willing, and ——————— .
Fair, fat, and ——————— .
Give, devise, and ——————— .

Variation

The game can also be played with sets of two, like *nip* and *tuck*, *time* and *tide*, *fame* and *fortune*, *fair* and *foul*, etc.

III

Alphabet and Spelling Games

Alphabetical Adverbs with Charades

Elementary-Intermediate

3 or more

This game has many educational values. It introduces the child to adverbs, it fosters creativity and inventiveness, and it builds vocabulary.

How to Play

Begin with a sentence containing an active verb that can be modified by a series of adverbs. These must be added by each player in turn, in alphabetical order, but in a way that makes sense.

Here is one possible start:

"The pilot flew the plane ——————."
Player 1: *A*crobatically.
Player 2: *B*umpily.
Player 3: *C*arelessly.
Player 1: *D*angerously.
Player 2: *E*nthusiastically.
Player 3: *F*rantically.

Before revealing his word, each player, with gestures or pantomine, acts it out, and the other players try to guess what it is, using as their clue the initial letter and the charade.

Alliterative Add-a-Word

Elementary-Intermediate

Paper and pencil

3 or more

Timer

This game helps children to appreciate the many ways in which the same initial letter can combine with others to form different sounds and words.

How to Play

The first player begins a sentence. Each player will add one word. Thus, if adjectives are being added in a sentence, the description might look something like this:

"Jane is —————."

Player 1:   Artful.
Player 2:   Able.
Player 3:   Alert.
Player 1:   Attentive.
Player 2:   Active.
Player 3:   Amiable.

Each player is given only a limited amount of time to think of another word to add to this list. When no one can do so, a new list is begun with the next letter of the alphabet.

Many new words can be learned in this way, and if they are written on a sheet of paper, the children can learn their spelling as well.

Variation

ADD-A-WORD can also become an excellent device for training the memory and teaching a child to concentrate if each player is required, before adding his own word, to recite the entire list from the beginning. In that case, the person who keeps score also keeps the list in writing for reference.

Alliterative Categories

Elementary-Intermediate   *Blank cards*
3 or more   *Timer*

This game teaches children to group things logically and to find quickly the exact words they want.

Preparation

Prepare a set of alphabet cards with several sets of each letter.

How to Play

First, a category is announced or agreed upon. It may be anything familiar to the players — food, drinks, flowers, trees, countries, authors, people in the news, automobiles, presidents, etc. — and can be made as extensive or as restrictive as desired. For example, the category might be confined to things seen at the circus, on a trip to the country, a visit to the museum, etc.

The cards are first shuffled. Then a player draws one from the top of the deck at the same moment that a timer is started by the timekeeper. Within thirty seconds, the player must call out a word that begins with the given letter and is in the given category.

Suppose, for example, that food is the category. If the letter B is drawn, the player scores a point if he calls out in time a word like *bread, butter, baked beans,* or *beets.* Other players, having a little more time to think than the first player, receive credit for only half a point for each word they can add to his. Of course, if the first player is very quick, he may be able to call out more than one correct answer before time is up.

The game proceeds in this fashion, with the players taking turns in drawing cards from the pack.

Stringing Along

Elementary-Intermediate   *Timer*
2 *or more*

This game teaches spelling and vocabulary and trains the child's visual memory.

How to Play

The first player starts by naming any letter of the alphabet. Each player in turn must "string along" by adding one letter, either *before* or *after* those already called out, to form a word. The ever-growing necklace of words, formed by adding one letter at a time to either end, constitutes a challenge to keep building longer words by the same process.

Thus, a game might proceed from *i* to *it* to *pit* to *spit* and *spite,* or *rip, trip,* and *tripe.* Another might begin with *o* and go on to *on, one, tone* and *stone.* Still another might start with *a* and string along from *at* to *ate* to *late* to *plate.*

Variation

The game can be made more difficult by permitting a

letter to be inserted also anywhere in the middle of a word to form a new word. Thus, *pit* might be transformed into *pint*, then to *print*, and finally to *sprint*. Since this places a greater strain on the memory, more time should be allowed for each answer.

Cutting the String

Elementary-Intermediate   *Timer*
2 or more

This is the opposite of STRINGING ALONG, but it serves the same educational purpose.

How to Play
Beginning with a word like *pirate*, each player in turn must slice off one letter at either end or internally to make some smaller word.

Good words to start with are *honesty, spinet, trash, flown, hasty, spore, party, spare, twine, stint, swinger, whist, tramp, snowy,* and *marshy*.

Scrambled Letters

Elementary-Intermediate   *Paper and pencil*
2 or more   *Timer*

With this game, children can be given training in logical classification, practice in spelling, and a knowledge of the precise vocabulary of any particular subject.

How to Play

Begin by having the players decide on categories of interest to them (sports, cars, toys, colors, countries, authors, flowers, fruits, musical instruments, etc.).

Next, each player makes a list, in a given period of time, of all the words he can think of that are connected with any one of these categories.

Now the players scramble the letters of each of the words they have listed.

The first player then announces the category he has chosen and gives the scrambled letters of one of the words on his list. With these clues, the next player must unscramble the letters and form the correct word.

For example, suppose a player chooses the category of sports. His list of scrambled letters might look something like this:

SUSAHQ — SQUASH
TONABNIMD — BADMINTON
YERCARH — ARCHERY
TOAFLOLB — FOOTBALL
NALDHLAB — HANDBALL
RSCOEC — SOCCER
FLOG — GOLF
TOCQUER — CROQUET
BOTLSAFL — SOFTBALL
CINFNEG — FENCING
GIXNOB — BOXING
GONTONIGBAG — TOBOGGANING
KNITAGS — SKATING
SLABELBA — BASEBALL
CEOYHK — HOCKEY
KAEBSTLBLA — BASKETBALL
RSAECOLS — LACROSSE

EBDULHFAFSRO — SHUFFLEBOARD
DLRABLSII — BILLIARDS
EBVYLAOLLL — VOLLEYBALL
SGWTNIERL — WRESTLING
IENTNS — TENNIS
LOOP — POLO
NLWBIOG — BOWLING

Since a player is likely to select first his longest and most difficult set of scrambled letters to present to his neighbor for unscrambling, the number of letters in the word can be used on a basis for crediting points. Thus, a player who successfully unscrambles the word *ebdulhfafsro* would get twelve points, while the player who unscrambles *loop* would get only four points. If a player misses, he earns no points, but he remains in the game.

To add to the interest, a time limit can be set for unscrambling the letters.

Word Ladders

All Levels   *Paper and pencil*
1 or more, or a large group

Children often fail to see the difference in spelling between words that look alike except for a single letter. This is an excellent game for sharpening their powers of observation and helping them to notice the effect of small differences between the spelling of one word and that of another.

How to Play

A child can play the game by himself, taking all the time he needs to climb to the top of the word ladder; or, if he has a companion, the two of them might compete to see who can reach the top in the fewest steps. In fact, a whole group could play the game at the same time.

The top and bottom rungs of the word ladder are two words of equal length that are related to each other in some way, either as antonyms (*love-hate, rich-poor, wet-dry, black-white, lose-find,* etc.) or as complements (*boy-man, seek-find*). The problem is to pass from the lowest rung of the ladder to the highest in the fewest number of steps by changing only one letter at a time to make a new word.

Thus, to pass from *boy* to *man* with very few intermediate steps, we might proceed as follows:

MAN
BAN
BAY
BOY

To change from *dry* to *wet,* we could follow this sequence:

WET
MET
MAT
MAY
DAY
DRY

The player passing from the lowest rung to the highest with the fewest number of changes wins the game.

It should be easy to pass from *him* to *her* and from *pot* to *pan* in a single intermediate step, from *wood* to *coal, fair* to *foul, frock* to *cloak, love* to *hate,* and *foal* to *colt* in two intermediate steps, and from *seek* to *find, find* to *lose,* and *warm* to *cold* in three intermediate steps.

Generally, in a three-letter word, the changes are not hard to make; but with words of four or five letters, it may be necessary to make as many as a dozen or more changes to climb to the top of the ladder. Thus, the game can be made progressively difficult by adding to the number of letters in the original words.

A point worth noting is that in going from a word like *fish* to a word like *clam*, one must find a way of shifting the sequence of the two inner letters from vowel-consonant to consonant-vowel. A good way of effecting this change is to form one or more intermediate words with a double vowel, or two vowels, in the middle.

This, for example, is the way we might make the transition from *fish* to *clam* in ten steps:

CLAM
CLAD
CLOD
CLOT
COOT
COLT
COST
CAST
FAST
FIST
FISH

Here are some good sets of words to begin and end word ladders: *rich-poor* (in eight steps), *black-green* (eight steps), *lead-gold* (in just *three* easy steps!), *soup-nuts* (five steps), *slow-fast* (seven steps), *sick-well* (four steps), *heat-cold* (four steps), and *eye-ear* (three steps). It is even possible to go from *easy* to *hard* in five steps, to pass from *less* to *more* in four steps, to change *rain* to *snow* in seven steps, and to make *flour* into *bread* in six steps. After a while the players might like to try changing *fail* to *pass*.

What you can't do with words!

Spelling Grab Bag

Elementary-Intermediate   *Blank cards*

2 or more

The words most frequently misspelled are common ones like *divide, among, believe, forty, separate, truly, until, similar, woman, writing, library, ninety, occasion, piece, grammar, disappoint, describe, coming,* etc. This game can be used to help children to learn the spelling of these and many other everyday words.

Preparation

Prepare a set of cards on each of which is written a phonetic respelling of some ordinary word which you would like the players to learn how to spell. For example, your cards might look like this: RUF, KWIK, VU, KOF, KAJI, AJASENT, AWKID, SKWOSH, ORENJ, MUSKITO, DUZ, FAWTH, SED, KONSHENS, CONKER, etc. The number of cards will depend on the number of players.

How to Play

Shuffle the cards and throw them into a box or bag. Each player then draws a card blindly from the bag when his turn comes, pronounces the word, and spells it correctly. If he misses, the next player gets a chance to spell the same word. When only two or three play this game, a point is scored for each letter of a correctly spelled word. If a larger group plays, those who misspell a word are eliminated, as in a spelling bee, and the one who finally "survives" wins the game.

Words for the game can be taken from those misspelled by the players in previous games or class spelling lists.

Spelling Duel

All Levels   *Timer*
2 only

This is a spelling review carried on between two players.

Preparation

Each player is given a list of ten words of approximately equal difficulty.

How to Play

Each player alternately "flings" (calls) some word from his list at his dueling antagonist. Three seconds is the time limit for each word. The referee must not only keep time but also check to see that words are properly pronounced and spelled.

One point is given for each correct spelling. When all twenty words have been completed, the duelists exchange "swords" — i.e., their lists of words. This time half a point is given for each correct spelling. The players keep exchanging the same list until both spell every word correctly within the allotted time. Then a new list is given to each. The player who accumulates the greatest number of points wins the game.

The game can be complicated by making the lists longer — say, twenty words — and by including ever more difficult words.

Spelling Bee Without the Sting

All Levels   *Timer*
Large groups

This is the ideal way of teaching the spelling "demons" — the words that almost everyone has trouble with. The words used can be graduated in difficulty to suit the abilities of the group.

How to Play

The players are arranged in a semicircle around the moderator and take turns spelling each word as it is given to them. Ten seconds are allowed for each answer. If a player spells his word correctly, the next player is given another word. If the player misspells the word, the next player is given the same word. This word is repeated until someone spells it correctly. Players who misspell words are eliminated, and the last "survivor" wins the round.

Variations

1. Another method of conducting a spelling bee is to give a player one point for each word he spells correctly and to let him proceed as far as he can down the list until he misses. Then his score is totaled, and the next player begins by trying to spell the word missed by the player before him. When the game is played in this way, the words in the list should be of relatively equal difficulty. At the end, the player with the greatest number of points wins the game.

2. Still another method of holding a spelling bee is to divide the players into two evenly matched teams, each sitting or standing in a line facing the other. Players alternate spelling words, with the first speller on Team A

followed by the first speller on Team B, until everyone on each team has had a chance. Players who misspell a word are eliminated from their team, until one team has been entirely eliminated.

3. Finally, a spelling bee may be conducted in such a way as to require the player on the opposite team to call immediately "Right!" or "Wrong!" on hearing a word spelled by his adversary. If he calls a correctly spelled word wrong or an incorrectly spelled word right, he is eliminated just as if he himself had misspelled a word. Thus, either or both of the opponents may be eliminated on the same word.

Letter Alone

Elementary   *Pencil and Paper*
Large groups   *Timer*

This is just a fun game with the alphabet.

How to Play

Give the players about five minutes to make up as many questions as they can to which the answer, in each case, is a single letter of the alphabet. After time is up, the first player asks his first question. The second player has only five seconds to give the answer. If he has the same question on his own list, he crosses it off and proceeds to ask the next player a different question.

One point is scored for each correct answer. No points are scored for errors or for failure to supply a question or an answer or for repeating a question or for not meeting the time limit.

Here is how such a game might proceed:

Player 1:		What letter asks a question?
Player 2:	Y.	What letter is a sheep?
Player 3:	U.	What letter is a person having fun?
Player 4:	U.	What letter is a vegetable?
Player 5:	P.	What letter is a signal or a clue?
Player 6:	Q.	What letter is a verb expressing debt?
Player 1:	O.	What letter is an exclamation of surprise?
Player 2:	O.	What letter is a large body of water?
Player 3:	C.	What letter is a bird?
Player 4:	J.	What letter is a long line?
Player 5:	Q.	What letter is a slang expression?
Player 6:	G.	What letter is an organ of the body?
Player 1:	I.	What letter refers to yourself?
Player 2:	I.	What letter is a beverage?
Player 3:	T.	What letter is an insect?
Player 4:	B.	

Letter Pair-Off

Elementary-Intermediate   *Paper and pencil*
Large groups   *Timer*

This variation of LETTER ALONE is a little more difficult and may be played after the possibilities of LETTER ALONE seem to have been exhausted.

How to Play

In this game the players must think up questions to

which the answer, in each instance, consists of two letters of the alphabet.

Here is how one such game might proceed:

Player 1: What two letters mean too much?

Player 2: XS. What two letters can mean whatever you mean?

Player 3: NE. What two letters mean a creeping vine?

Player 4: IV. What two letters mean a message received by cable?

Player 5: YR. What two letters mean cautious, crafty, cunning?

Player 6: KG. What two letters refer to a county in England?

Player 1: SX. What two letters mean shabby?

Player 2: CD. What two letters refer to your vision?

Player 3: IC. What two letters refer to my vision?

Player 4: UC. What two letters are a man's name?

Player 5: ON. What two letters are not difficult at all?

Player 6: EZ. What two letters would you use when you have scraped the bottom of the barrel?

Player 1: MT. What two letters refer to a doll?

Player 2: QP. What two letters would you use as a term of affection?

Player 3: QT. What two letters are a number?

Player 4: AT. What two letters mean to surpass?

Player 5: XL.

There are, of course, many other two-letter combinations, like *bd, pt, rt, ln, le, lc, kt, me, dk, tp, sa, nv,* etc., that can be used in this game, to say nothing of repeated letters like *t*'s and *e*'s and *y*'s and *u*'s.

Choosy

This is a game that encourages creativity and imagination, places a premium on a good memory, and teaches spelling.

How to Play

The leader begins by announcing, "I am collecting contributions for Choosy _____ [here inserting his or her own name — say, Jane], who detests *ease*. What will you give Choosy Jane?"

Each player must in turn name a gift for Choosy Jane that does not have the letter E in it. If he names a gift that has already been mentioned or that contains the letter E, he is eliminated.

Here is how the game might proceed:

Leader: What will you give Choosy Jane?
Player 1:   A sword.
Leader: And what will you give her?
Player 2:   A belt.
Leader: You're out. There is an *e* in "belt." What will you give her?
Player 3:   A gun.
Leader: And what will you give her?
Player 4:   A new red hat.
Leader: You're out. There is an *e* in "new" and another in "red." What will you give her?
Player 5:   A gun.
Leader: You're out. She already has a gun. What will you give her?

After one time around, contributions may be solicited for someone who does not like bees. Thereafter, gifts can be restricted to meet the special tastes of a Choosy who does not like seas, eyes, jays, ells, ems, ens, peas, cues, or teas.

If the leader fails to spot a mistake made by one of the other players, he loses his position, and another player takes his place.

Variations

1. Once the players have had a chance to develop their technique, they may try to please a particularly choosy Choosy who dislikes *both* ease and eyes. In this way, the game can be made increasingly difficult.

2. This game can also be used to teach the specialized vocabulary of any subject and the spelling of the words connected with it. For example, Choosy could be a musician who detests the wise and has no taste for peas or ease. It may then take some imagination and ingenuity to think of gifts that would be suitable for him. Similarly, whether Choosy is about to go on a trip to Europe, or is a sailor, a soldier, a baseball player, or an astronaut, his special needs will always have to be satisfied with gifts that take account of his peculiar likes and dislikes.

IV

Grammar and

Sentence-Construction Games

Word Painting

All Levels
3 or more

Blank cards
Timer

This game emphasizes the function of the adjective as a modifier of a noun. It trains the memory and builds vocabulary at the same time.

Preparation

A deck of cards is prepared with a number of nouns selected by the teacher in accordance with the abilities and interests of the players — e.g., *monkey, name, magician, bicycle, mountain, intrusion, greeting, inquiry,* and *home.* The pack is then shuffled and laid face down on the table.

How to Play

The first player, drawing the top card of the pack, holds it up for the other players to see. He must now suggest, within a given time, some adjective that will "paint" the noun. Thus, if he has drawn *home,* he may say, "Happy home."

Now the next player must think of another adjective to paint the same noun — perhaps *unhappy* or *convalescent.* The game proceeds in this fashion until a player either repeats some adjective that has already been given, proposes an unsuitable adjective, or cannot think of another adjective within the time limit. It then becomes his turn to pick the next card from the top of the pack and to begin another round.

Players score one point for each correct adjective and lose two points for each miss or fumble.

Variations

1. One way of making the game more difficult as well as instructive is to require that each player give *two* appropriate adjectives to paint each noun — e.g., *polite, persistent inquiry; amusing, fictitious name; loud, hearty greeting;* etc. This is a good way of teaching the use of precise, vivid language.

2. The game can also be made more challenging by beginning with a deck that includes cards with nouns for which there are relatively limited range of appropriate modifiers, like *nourishment, sickle, ownership, audition, breadth, compatriot,* etc. Of course, the time limit would have to be adjusted with the increase in difficulty.

3. Finally, the procedure can be reversed: the words written on the cards may all be adjectives — in effect, different kinds of "paint" — and the players may be invited to use them to draw different pictures. In this case too, it is possible to pass from relatively easy types of adjectives, like *good, clean, smooth,* etc., to those more difficult.

Everyday Grammar

Intermediate

2 or more

In this game, the attention is focused on the vocabulary of everyday life, but with the object of learning the parts of speech and seeing how they function in ordinary language.

How to Play

The players begin by agreeing on a particular area of everyday experience that they would like to talk about — e.g., baseball, school, home, etc. Then they agree on a particular part of speech to start with — say, verbs. Each player, in turn, must now say something, in a complete sentence, about the subject agreed upon, but using a verb specifically suited to it. Thus, if the first player had to use a verb in a sentence about boxing, he might say, "The champion *feinted* with his left." The story of the entire fight must then be told with a different verb in each successive sentence:

Player 2: The challenger *countered* with a hard right to the jaw.

Player 3: His opponent *jabbed* lightly with his left.

A verb, once used, may not be repeated.

After a game like this, the average student will probably remember that a verb expresses *action*.

Variation

In the same way, sentences can be made up with adjectives or adverbs to tell a whole story — of a ballgame, a day at school, or a trip to the dentist. Besides teaching grammar, this game stimulates imagination and develops the ability to shape complete sentences.

Grammar Rummy

Intermediate-Advanced   *Blank cards*
2 or more

This game teaches the child to recognize the most important parts of speech and the essential elements of a sentence; to make verbs agree in number with their simple or compound subjects; to use the parts of speech to build sentences with subject, predicate, and modifiers; and to develop "sentence sense" — i.e., the ability to distinguish between a whole sentence and a fragment.

Preparation

1. Fifty-two cards will be needed to make a complete deck. Each card will have a word written on it. On ten of them write nouns (*truck, cousin,* etc.); on ten, verbs (*honked, walk,* etc.); on seven, phrases (*to the house, in the street,* etc.); on nine, articles (*a, an, the* — three of each); on six, conjunctions (*and, but, or* etc.); and on ten, adjectives (*big, white,* etc.).

2. Next shuffle, cut, deal, and play, following the rules of rummy. In a two-handed game, ten cards are dealt, one at a time, to each player; in a three-handed game, seven cards; and when four or more play, six cards. The next card is then placed, face up, beside the rest of the deck, which is laid face down.

How to Play

Each player in turn must *either* draw a card from the

top of the deck, without showing it, *or* take the card that is lying face up beside the deck. When adding the new card to his hand, he must discard one from it, laying it face up on top of the one already face up. Only the top card may be drawn from either of the two piles.

Whenever a player has put together a complete sentence, he lays on the table, face up, all the cards forming the sentence. After drawing and discarding, any player may eliminate a card from his hand by adding it meaningfully to some sentence already laid down by another player.

The object of the game is to be the first to eliminate all the cards in one's hand by laying them out in sentences. Or the rules can be modified to require the laying out of sets of nouns, verbs, adjectives, phrases, etc.

Variations

1. The parts of speech may be selected to exemplify different *types* of each — common and proper nouns (*house, John*); abstract and concrete nouns (*bravery, button*); singular and plural nouns (*family, friends*); transitive, intransitive, and copulative verbs (*remember, live, is*); active and passive verbs (*move, was taken*); present, past, and future tenses of verbs (*likes, enjoyed, will come*); regular and irregular verbs (*walked, fought*); singular and plural verbs (*has, have*); conjunctions (*or, because*), etc.

2. Then too, the pack of cards can be enlarged to include pronouns in various cases (*I, him, their,* us) and adverbs (*slowly, here*). Or the proportions of the different parts of speech in the total "mix" can be varied.

3. Finally, the words written on the cards can be selected from particular fields, like sports or the arts for

nouns, or from categories, like colors, shapes, sizes, and numbers for adjectives.

Gram-o

Elementary-Intermediate
3 or more

Blank cards (bingo size)
Small clips of paper
Small colored cardboard squares

This game, which is very similar to bingo, is an excellent way of reviewing the parts of speech. The materials needed require some preparation; but once they have been produced, they can be used over and over again.

Preparation

1. Each participant receives a card like the one shown below. Except for the top line, all the cards are different.

2. In addition, the players receive a number of small

G	R	A	M	O
NOUN	ADVERB	PROPER NOUN	ADJ.	PRONOUN
ADJ.	PREP.	ADVERB	NOUN	VERB
ADJ.	PRONOUN	FREE SPACE	ADVERB	NOUN
VERB	ADJ.	VERB	PREP.	ADVERB
PREP.	NOUN	ADJ.	VERB	PREP.

colored squares of cardboard that can be placed over the boxes on the card.

3. Slips of paper are prepared, each containing a letter of the word GRAM-O followed by a word representing a particular part of speech — for example, A-LITTLE.

How to Play

From a box into which these slips have been placed the leader picks one and reads it to the group. Let us say he selects A-LITTLE. All the players now check their cards to see whether they have a box labeled ADJECTIVE in the row under the letter A. (In the particular card shown here, it is the lowest box in the row.) Whoever has such a box writes the word on one of his colored cardboard squares and places it over the box on his card.

The game proceeds in this way until one of the players has covered a whole row horizontally, vertically, or diagonally. He then calls out "Gram-o" and steps up to have his card checked. Of course, he gets no credit if he incorrectly identifies the part of speech of any of the words he has claimed credit for. Thus, GRAM-O is not simply a game of chance; it calls for a knowledge of grammar as well as a certain amount of good luck.

Variation

The game can be made more interesting if the words that are chosen are capable of being used as more than one part of speech. For example, *well* can be a noun, an adjective, an interjection, or an adverb, depending upon its usage. To narrow down the possibilities in such cases, the word may be given in a sentence, so that the players must determine its part of speech from the way in which it is used.

Sentence Ghost

Intermediate-Advanced   *Timer*

2 or more

Children playing this game should be familiar with the classic game of GHOST (page 31), of which it is a variation.

SENTENCE GHOST develops the ability to recognize a sentence, to determine when a sentence ends, and to expand and develop a sentence with phrases and clauses. In fact, this game can be used to teach the whole art of constructing sentences of different types:

Declarative — one which makes a statement, like "John is a good sport."

Interrogative — one which asks a question, like "Is John a good sport?"

Imperative — one which expresses a command, like "John, be a good sport."

Exclamatory — one which exclaims, like "What a good sport John is!"

How to Play

The first player, thinking of a sentence of more than two words, calls out just its first word. Then the second player, thinking perhaps of the same sentence or of some other sentence of at least three words, adds a second word. Each succeeding player must think of a sentence that begins with the words already called out and must add one word, but *he must avoid completing any sentence*.

Generally, only one minute is allowed for a player either to add a word or to challenge the preceding player to say what sentence he had in mind. If the preceding player cannot meet this challenge, either because he really had no sentence in mind or because what he had in mind did not constitute a sentence, he is penalized by becoming a fifth of a ghost. If he does meet the challenge, then it is his challenger who is penalized, as in GHOST. A player suffers the same penalty if he completes a sentence of three or more words and someone else points this out.

A second penalty makes a player two fifths of a ghost, etc. The other rules of GHOST apply to this game as well.

The tendency of the game is to encourage the players to lengthen sentences by adding adjectives and adverbs.

Grammar Ghost

Intermediate-Advanced   *Timer*
2 or more

This is a good game for reviewing the parts of speech, adding to the players' vocabulary, and improving their spelling.

How to Play

The rules are the same as those for GHOST (page 31), except that the words must all belong to the same part of speech.

For example, suppose it is agreed that all the words are to be adjectives. The first player thinks of some adjective consisting of more than three letters, for example *short*. He calls out the first letter, in this case S. Then the second player, thinking of some other adjective or perhaps of the same one, adds a second letter, say H, which might also help to spell *sharp*. Now each succeeding player must think of an adjective that begins with the same letters that have already been called out and must add one letter, but he must avoid completing any word.

As in GHOST, a minute is allowed for a player either to add a letter without completing a word or to challenge the preceding player to say what word he had in mind. The penalties are the same as in GHOST.

Variation

The game can be varied so that all the parts of speech except articles — nouns, verbs, pronouns, interjections, adverbs, prepositions, and conjunctions — can be covered as well as adjectives.

Scrambled Sentence

Elementary-Intermediate   *Blank cards*
1 or more

This is a very simple game that teaches the players how to put words together to form sentences, to punctuate correctly, and to connect ideas intelligibly.

How to Play

According to the age and maturity of the players, select some saying, quotation, or proverb, or make up a sentence on any subject like history or geography. For example, the sentence might describe a person, an animal, a place, or a thing, or it might be a familiar advertising slogan or a statement of some well-known fact of history or common experience.

Break the sentence up into a succession of words and write these on cards. Make a duplicate set of cards for each player.

Now shuffle each set so that the sentence is thoroughly scrambled in every case.

The first player to put the sentence together wins the game.

Coffeepot

Advanced
Large groups

This old favorite is a grammatical variation of the game of TEAKETTLE (page 46). It teaches the players the correct use of different parts of speech, broadens their vocabulary, and stimulates imagination as well as much laughter. The larger the group, the more fun it is to play.

How to Play

One of the players volunteers or is chosen by lot to be the "victim." While he is out of the room, the rest of the group agrees on some verb, like *talk, sing, eat, dance, smile, loaf*, etc., to be represented by the word "coffeepot."

When the victim returns, he asks questions of the players in rotation, using "coffeepot" to stand for the verb, in an effort to find out what it is. It is his job to devise questions that will lead him to the verb in the shortest possible time. The players must answer his questions truthfully in accordance with the meaning of the verb they have chosen.

Suppose, for example, that the verb *sing* has been selected. The interrogation might proceed as follows:

Q. Can everyone coffeepot?
A. Well, that depends on what you call coffeepotting.
Q. Can you coffeepot with other people?
A. Oh, yes.

Q. Can you coffeepot alone?
A. Yes, indeed.
Q. Do you need special equipment to coffeepot?
A. No special outfit is needed, if that's what you mean.

The game proceeds in this way until the victim guesses what the verb is. He is penalized one point for every wrong guess and for every question he has to ask before he guesses right. The next victim is the one who has given the answer that enabled the first victim to guess the correct verb.

Grammar ABC's

Elementary-Intermediate   *Blank cards*
Large groups   *Timer*

This game is a pleasant way of reviewing the parts of speech.

Preparation
Prepare two decks of fifty-two cards each by attaching removable stickers to them. On each sticker write a letter of the alphabet according to the following plan: nine E's, seven each of A's, I's, O's, U's, and Y's, and three each of the consonants.

How to Play
After shuffling the deck thoroughly, the first player says to the second, "I have a message for you from a friend of yours."

"Whom?" asks the second player.

The first player now turns up the top card in the deck.

Suppose it is the letter F. The first player answers the question using an appropriate adjective beginning with the letter on the card drawn from the deck. He might say, "I have forgotten his name, but he has a *funny* face." Player 1 now keeps his F card.

Next, the second player draws a card from the top of the deck — say, M — and asks, for example, "Did he have a *monkey* face?" Or he may use any other appropriate adjective beginning with that letter. He too keeps his card with M.

The game continues in this way until everyone has had a chance to draw a card and answer the sentence using an appropriate adjective beginning with the letter drawn. No duplication of adjectives is allowed. Thus, if another F is drawn, the player who turns up this card must supply some adjective other than funny to describe the friend's face — perhaps *freckled, fat,* or *flushed.*

If all the players are able to supply appropriate *adjectives* the first time around, they proceed to use *nouns* in the second round. The first player, when his turn comes again, might begin by saying, "Your friend brought with him a _____ ." He now draws a card from the top of the deck — say, letter B — and fills in a noun beginning with that letter — e.g., basketball. The next player, saying, "He also brought a _____ ," must do likewise with the letter he draws, and so must the rest of the players.

In the third round, *adverbs* are sought. Thus, the first player might begin the round by stating, "Your friend was dressed _____ ."

Here a P might appropriately be used for *plainly.* In each round, the form of the statement or question is determined by the first player and is followed by the others.

In the fourth round, *verbs* are in demand. Hence, the

statement may take the form: "Your friend _____ when he came." Here the letter Y might be used to form the verb *yawned*.

If a player cannot think of an appropriate word, within a given time, he is penalized one point and passes his letter to the next player, who tries to provide a word beginning with it. Each player accumulates in a pile in front of him the letters with which he provided suitable words.

Variations

1. To make the game more challenging, players may be forbidden to introduce words that make sentences contradicting what has already been said by other players. Thus, if one player says that the friend's face was *kind*, it would be inappropriate for another player to describe it as *mean*, *cruel*, or *evil*.

2. The form of the questions or statements may be changed in order to encourage a broader range of possible sentences. It is a good idea to list beforehand questions and replies requiring different parts of speech, perhaps building up a story or situation to a climax. For instance, in one game a person met a *wicked* man who turned out to be a *robber* who laughed *sinisterly* and *stole* a bunch of jewels.

This game provides many opportunities for humorous or exaggerated use of language in the creation of sentences.

Taboo

Intermediate   *Timer*
Large groups

Playing this game will develop verbal facility, alertness,

and an appreciation of the way the parts of speech are used in sentences.

How to Play

First, a questioner is chosen. Then, it is agreed that a particular part of speech — say, the noun — is to be taboo for everyone but him. He may use as many nouns as he likes in asking questions of each of the players in turn, but they must avoid nouns in their answers. He is free to ask any questions he wants in an effort to trap a player into using the forbidden part of speech. Anyone who does so is "out."

Here is how the questioning might begin:

Q. How do you like this game?

A. I think it's a good game.

Q. You're out! You used the noun "game"! If you wanted to chop down a tree, what instrument would you use?

A. I'd use whatever I could find that was handy.

Q. What is that you're wearing around your neck?

A. Call it what you may, it's not knotted, but beaded. Haven't I identified it precisely?

Q. I'll ask the questions. Which do you like better, day or night?

A. Neither.

After one time around, a new part of speech may be made taboo: the adjective, the conjunction, the preposition, the pronoun. In each case the problem is different, and it takes quite as much proficiency to frame the questions as it does to find an appropriate answer.

Here is how a questioner might try to trap players into using verbs:

Q. What do you do when you are embarrassed?
A. Nothing in particular.
Q. How would you react if you saw a ghost?
A. Calmly, without fear or agitation.
Q. What must a person do to keep in good health?
A. Everything necessary for nutrition, exercise, and rest.

A time limit should be set on responses.

Stuff and Nonsense

Elementary-Intermediate
Large groups

This is a good game for teaching children the way the parts of speech are used in the construction of sentences. It is best played with a group of at least eight. More can join if the game is suitably modified.

How to Play

The players are seated in a circle. One starts by whispering to his neighbor at his left an article (*a, an,* or *the*). The player thus spoken to then whispers to the one at his left an adjective (*sick, young, ugly,* etc.). The third player must whisper to his neighbor a singular noun (*fool, dog, song,* etc.). Each player, in turn, adds another part of speech and passes it along to the person at his left, in the following order thereafter: verb, adverb, a number, another adjective, and a plural noun.

When the eighth player has been reached, all take turns, in order, calling out the words they contributed, until the complete sentence is heard. The result can be very funny. For example, one group came up with the following: "The aggressive motorman carved morosely sixty-nine silly cats."

Variations

The game can be complicated by changing the order of the parts of speech; adding conjunctions (*or, and,* etc.) and interjections (*ouch, well, ah*); or specifying a particular kind of pronoun (personal — *he, me, us;* relative — *which, who, that;* or interrogative — *whose, whom*) or adjective (color, shape, size, etc.). In this way children can be taught the various kinds of sentences, clauses, and phrases.

Sentence Treasure Hunt

Elementary-Intermediate   *Paper and pencil*
Large groups   *Blank cards*

This is an "action" game for a group of children who won't sit still for very long. It will develop their ability to see words and phrases as functional parts of the sentence; to connect and arrange them meaningfully, logically, and grammatically; and to recognize well-known expressions or sayings.

Preparation

Take some famous quotation, nursery rhyme, proverb, advertising slogan, or poem, and divide it into a number of words and phrases. Write these on separate slips or cards and hide them under erasers, behind the blinds, or in various nooks and crannies around the classroom.

How to Play

When the children assemble, send them out on a hunt to find the hidden "treasure."

If a player comes upon a word or a phrase, he is to leave it just where he found it, and copy it on a sheet of paper without saying anything. He then moves on in search of the other parts of the original quotation or poem until he has put them all together. The first to do so wins.

The difficulty of the game can be varied according to the length and complexity of the passage selected.

Index of Skills Taught

This index will enable you to select the specific skill you wish to have your students develop and the game or games best suited to teach it.